They Must Not Be Forgotten:

Heroic Priests And Nuns Who Saved People From The Holocaust

By

Sally M. Rogow

Cover design by: Jay Cookingham

Copyright © 2005 Sally M. Rogow

ISBN: 0-9767211-6-3

Published by:
Holy Fire Publishing
531 Constitution Blvd. Martinsburg, WV 25401
www.ChristianPublish.com

Printed in the United States of America and the United Kingdom

Ackmowledgement

The author is grateful to the many individuals who encouraged, inspired and provided information for the writing of this book.

Very special thanks to Reverend Vincent Lapomarda, distinguished scholar and coordinator of Holocaust research at the College of the Holy Cross, who took the time to edit some of the stories and make many helpful suggestions.

Archbishop Raymond Roussin of Vancouver, British Columbia, encouraged the writing of this book and put me in touch with Father John Horgan who gave me valuable source materials.

Valuable material was also supplied by the research staff of Yad Vashem, the Holocaust Martyrs' and Heroes' Remembrance Authority in Israel which is dedicated to remembrance, documentation, education and research.

Solly Kaplinski, Director of the English Desk in the International Relations Division of Yad Vashem gave his enthusiastic support and put me in touch with the research staff who supplied important documents.

Books and articles by Dr. Mordechai Paldiel, Director of the Righteous Among The Nations Department at Yad Vashem were rich sources of information.

The encouragement and support of family and friends is also very gratefully acknowledged.

Content

Introduction

This century has witnessed an unspeakable tragedy, which can never be forgotten: the attempt by the Nazi regime to exterminate the Jewish people with the consequent killing of millions of Jews, women, men, old and young children and infants, for the sole reason of their Jewish origin were persecuted and deported. Some were killed immediately, while others were tortured and utterly robbed of their human dignity and then murdered."

Cardinal Edward Idris Cassidy (1998)

The systematic murder of Jewish people that took place under Hitler's rule is called the Holocaust. It was a sadistic and planned campaign of mass extermination. In every country occupied by the Germans, Jewish people were arrested, deported and sent to death camps. Of the 9 million Jewish people who lived in Europe at the beginning of World War II, only a fraction survived the Holocaust. Six million Jewish people perished and five million others, including Gypsies, people with disabilities, German youth who opposed Hitler, Polish prisoners, Jehovah's Witnesses, and resistance fighters.

The Holocaust took place under a brutal and powerful dictatorship in possession of an advanced technology in the midst of war. Many people wonder how a civilized nation could carry out such a barbaric genocide. The Holocaust could not have happened if people refused to tolerate prejudice, and the isolating and demeaning of people because of religion, race, disability, or other differences. The lessons of the Holocaust teach the dangers of prejudice and lack of respect for human life.

The heroism and the goodness of those who refused to sit by and do nothing in the face of merciless persecution need to be acknowledged and celebrated. This book tells the stories of heroic Catholic priests and nuns who risked their lives to rescue Jewish people from the Holocaust. Rescue was dangerous and difficult. The Nazi Gestapo and secret police were vigilant and quick to punish anyone who tried to save Jewish people.

Renzo De Felice, an Italian historian, calculated that 155 Catholic institutions, convents and monasteries, orphan homes, institutions and hospitals in Italy opened their doors to Jewish refugees and made it possible for the majority of Italian Jews to be saved from the Holocaust. In France, close to 12,000 children were saved by priests and nuns. Cardinal Henri de Lubac (1896-1991), a Jesuit priest, wrote about the efforts of many French priests to resist the Nazi racial laws and rescue Jewish people. In spite of the fact that in Poland, assistance to Jewish people was a crime punishable by death, there were priests and nuns who hid Jewish children.

In the midst of terror, persecution, and grave danger, these heroic priests and nuns were true to their belief in the sanctity of human life and took action. The priests and nuns whose stories are told in this book have been recognized and honored as the "Righteous among The Nations" by the Yad Vashem, the Holocaust Martyrs and Heroes Remembrance Authority, established in 1953 by the government of Israel. Trees have been planted in their honor in the Garden of the Righteous.

As Pope John Paul II noted in a tribute ceremony at the Yad Vashem, *The honour given to the just gentiles' by the State of Israel at Yad Vashem for having acted heroically to save Jews, sometimes to the point of giving their own lives, is a recognition that not even in the darkest hour is every light extinguished."*

The Catholic church has also recognized and honored these priests and nuns.

A Courageous Rescue: The Story of Assisi.

Assisi, a medieval town 70 miles north of Rome, is the birthplace of St. Francis, the patron saint of Italy. During World War II, Italy fought with the Germans and surrendered to the United States and Great Britain in 1943. German troops stormed into northern Italy and began the persecution of Italian Jews who had lived peacefully with their neighbors for centuries.

Hundreds of people whose homes had been destroyed in bombing raids were coming to Assisi to find refuge. The Germans declared Assisi a "hospital city" and the Bishop of Assisi was ordered to turn over many buildings to be used as hospitals for wounded German soldiers.

In the middle of the night, Father Nicacci was awakened. Bishop Nicolini wanted to see him right away. He dressed quickly. It must be an urgent matter, why else would the Bishop summon him at midnight, he thought. The Bishop lived in a house behind the Church of Santa Maria Maggiore, a mile away.

Rufino Nicacci was a young priest who was appointed Father Guardian of the seminary of San Damiano the year before. He grew up in a farming village close to Assisi and knew the countryside. Taking the shortcut path, he walked quickly through low bushes and olive trees. The air was filled with the aroma of rosemary and woodbine and a chorus of cicados broke the silence of the night. The path led to a crooked alley behind the church.

As soon as he arrived at the Bishop's home, the Bishop greeted him. "It's so important that you came. What I have to tell you must be kept secret." The Bishop told him about the letter he received from the Pope describing the danger facing Jewish people. Whole families were being arrested, children were being taken from their parents, Jewish people were being taken to death and concentration camps.

Father Nicacci knew about the hundreds of refugees in Assisi fleeing from bombed out towns and villages in southern Italy. They were being looked after by Don Aldo Brunacci, the Canon of the Cathedral of San Rufino, but he did not know about the Jews.

How can I help, Father? Father Nicacci asked.

We have a group of Jewish people in the church. They just escaped from Rome and arrived this afternoon," the Bishop explained that Cardinal Boetto who worked with

14

the Jewish underground organization (DELASEM) and Father Dalla Costa, the Archbishop of Florence had arranged for their escape from Italy.

You will take them to Florence tonight. They must be there before dawn."

When do we leave? Father Nicacci asked the Bishop.

Everyone is ready. A basket of food has been prepared for you to take on the train."

A group of ten people came into the room. The young priest could see the fear in their eyes and spoke to them. "You have nothing to fear. We will walk to the train station, board a train and get to Florence safely." Father Nicacci sounded more confident than he felt. The trip was risky, there were German troops in Florence and more German soldiers were coming to Assisi every day.

Everyone was ready to go. An elderly man with a beard brought a suitcase to the Bishop. "Please Father, Would you hide the Torah scroll?" he pleaded and opened the suitcase. Inside there was a beautiful Torah scroll. The Torah contains the first five books of the Old Testament.

The elderly man was a Rabbi and brought the Torah from the synagogue in Rome.

Of course, the Bishop replied. The words of the Torah are also important to the church. I promise you it will be well hidden. " The Rabbi thanked him and carefully replaced the Torah in the suitcase and gave it to the Bishop.

Father Nicacci took the arm of elderly rabbi as they walked to the train station. The station was empty, there were no German soldiers around. He bought 11 tickets and they boarded the train to Florence. No sooner had they taken their seats when a detachment of German soldiers boarded the train. One of the soldiers shouted, "Show us your papers."

Father Nicacci knew that the refugees had no identification papers, he could only hope that the letter the Bishop wrote explaining that the group were pilgrims on their way to Florence, would satisfy the soldiers. He reached for the letter when he heard a loud blast. It was a bombing raid and British planes were overhead. The German soldiers turned around and jumped off the train.

The raid could not have come at a better time, Father Nicacci thought to himself as he watched the soldiers leaving.

When the train began to move, he passed the basket of food around.

Bless you Father; an elderly man whispered to him.

We are all to be blessed, he replied.

Everyone ate and chatted, until the train stopped in Florence. Inside the station, there were German guards. Father Nicacci made sure no one was stopped. Quickly and quietly, in groups of two and three, Father Nicacci led them to them to the church, where Father Dalla Costa was waiting. In a few hours the refugees would be on their way to Genoa. The mission was a success.

A few weeks later, the German army, secret police and the Gestapo set up road blocks and barricaded the gates of Assisi. A night curfew was imposed, any one found outside of their home after nightfall would be shot. The Germans also posted a warning that any one who participated in an act of sabotage or obstructed a military movement would be executed. It was no longer possible to get refugees out of the country.

Trucks filled with German soldiers were on the roads searching for resistance fighters and Jews. The Bishop called Father Nicacci again.

We have to find new hiding places. . The Germans have taken over the hotels and there are no public places where Jewish refugees can be hidden."

More Jewish refugees had come to Assisi, some were from eastern Europe and did not speak Italian. The only possible hiding places left were the convents where the nuns lived. The Bishop sent Father Nicacci to speak to Mother Guisseppina, the Mother Superior of the convent of the Poor Clares, to open the doors of the convent to the Jewish refugees.

These people are desperate and we have no other places to hide them," he told her.

You know we have never had men in the convent. We cannot take them without special permission from the Pope," Mother Guisseppina explained.

Father Nicacci knew it was useless to argue and went to talk to the Bishop, who came back to the church with him. The Bishop assured the Mother Superior that the Pope would

18

approve if she opened the doors of the convent to suffering people. She agreed to open the convent doors to the refugees and spoke to the other nuns.

Father Nicacci brought the refugees to the convent that afternoon. No sooner was the last person taken inside the convent, when he heard a car stop in front of the church and a loud knock on the door. Mother Guisseppina opened the door to a German officer with a gun in his hand.

How dare you enter the convent with a gun. Don't you know that it is only nuns who live here. I will not let you enter," she said in a stern voice, To everyone's relief, the officer left.

The nuns took good care of the refugees. They even prepared a kitchen so that those Jewish people who observed the dietary laws would be able to eat. Father Nicacci brought them robes and habits to wear and the Bishop arranged with a printer to prepare false identification papers. Don Brunacci set up a school for Jewish children so they would not fall behind in their school work and Father Nicacci taught them Catholic prayers so they would not be suspect in the church. With the identification cards, those refugees who spoke

Italian were allowed to leave the convent during the day, the others had to stay inside.

As more refugees arrived and the escape routes closed off, plans were made to transfer some refugees to monasteries in other towns. The monastery in Abruzzi, notified the Bishop that it would hide refugees. How they were to be transported was a problem. There were no vehicles that could be used to transport them. Abruzzi was many miles away.

Father Nicacci found himself very busy. He was the first to greet newcomers to the seminary. Colonel Mueller, the German doctor in charge of the medical services was a devout Catholic and came to San Damiano. Father Nicacci made him feel welcome. The Colonel was grateful and told him to call on him if he needed anything.

When the Bishop asked him to find a way to get the refugees to Abruzzi, Father Nicacci decided to take a big risk. He knew the Colonel had trucks at his disposal and he told him that a group of Italian pilgrims were having trouble getting back to Abruzzi. He asked the Colonel if he could help.

I don't see why not, Colonel Mueller replied and offered to send a truck.

The pilgrims are at the Bishop's church, Father Nicacci explained.

The Colonel sent a canvas covered truck to church with two German officers to make sure the truck would not be stopped at any of the checkpoints. Colonel Mueller came to the church himself to see that everything was in order. Two German soldiers with rifles slung across their backs would travel with them. They seemed happy to be of service.

Father Nicacci brought the refugees out to the truck. They were dressed in priestly robes. One of the men was a Rabbi. Father Nicacci sat beside the driver, feeling like an actor in a play, he acted calm and friendly and gave no hint of his fear. The truck had to stop at several checkpoints. When the guards saw the German soldiers, they waved it on.

It began to rain and the driver wanted to stop, but Father Nicacci calmly told him the pilgrims had to be at the monastery by morning. The truck drove through the night.

When they arrived at the monastery in Abruzzi, Father Nicacci helped the refugees get off the truck and shook their hands. When they were safely inside the monastery, he got back into the truck for the return trip.

My prayers have been answered, he thought to himself as he sat next to the driver. The soldiers did not speak Italian, but when the truck arrived back in Assisi, he shook their hands and thanked them warmly. . No one suspected the pilgrims were a group of Jewish refugees.

The monasteries and convents in Assisi were full of refugees. The Germans were becoming suspicious and decided to raid the monasteries and convents. The Bishop found out about the planned raids and warned Father Nicacci that the convent of Poor Clares was to be raided that afternoon. He raced to the convent and found everyone ready to leave. The sister had stripped the beds and made sure that nothing was around that would give them away.

"Follow me, " Father Nicacci told the refugees and led them down into a long underground passage. It was dark and several of the older people had to be helped through the dark tunnel. In some parts of the tunnel people had to crawl on their hands and knees.

At the end of the tunnel, they crawled out onto the steep mountainside covered with rocks. From there they went into the forest or into the cave on the hillside, where St. Francis had once lived. Father Nicacci took the old man he helped through the tunnel back to the seminary San Damiano.

Every cloister and convent in Assisi was searched. The Germans suspected Father Nicacci and arrested him. He was put into a prison and starved for three days. Father Nicacci refused to talk and was threatened with punishment. He knew he faced jail and possible torture, but he would not betray anyone and stayed silent. The Mayor of Assisi came to his defense and he was finally released.

In June 1944, Rome was liberated by the Allies and the German army retreated from Assisi. Not a single Jew who had been hidden in Assisi was arrested.

About 200 Jews remained in Assisi for the duration of the war. Father Brunacci remarked after the war, "In all about 300 Jews were entrusted to us by Divine Providence; with God's help, and through the intercession of St. Francis, not one of them fell into the hands of their persecutors."

After the war, Guiseppe Nicolini, Rufino Nicacci and Aldo Brunacci were honoured by the Yad Vashem, the Holocaust Documentation Center in Jerusalem, Israel. They were given gold medals and honored as "righteous among the nations. "

References

Encyclopedia of the Holocaust, 1990, Macmillan Publishing Company, NYC, NY 10022.

Marchione, Margharita, *Yours Is a Precious Witness: Memoirs of Jews and Catholics in Wartime Italy*, New York/Mahwah, N.J. Paulist Press, 1997

Ramati, Alexander, *While The Pope Kept Silent: Assisi and The Nazi Occupation* (as told by Padre Rufino Nicacci. London, England, George Allen and Unwin, 1978

Father Marie Benoit

To our dear Father Marie-Benoit

For having saved our own lives

And those of thousands of others,

Long live Pere Marie Benoit!

The brave priest who saved us,

The one who gave us courage,

The one who protected us,

Food he found, and clothing,

And shelter for the children

Long live Pere Marie Benoit!

For us he would have died,

For us he worked night and day,

Moved by a great love of God

To care for his unhappy children.

Long live Pere Marie-Benoit

To our children we shall tell tales

Of this great priest, this great hero

Who fought for us so mightily,

And by his love saved us all.

To us, you have been,

And always will remain,

Our most beloved father

(Tribute composed by the Jewish children of Rome Father
Benoit saved from the Nazis, (Leboucher, p.165)

Father Benoit was a leader of one of the most courageous rescue efforts that took place in Europe and saved the lives of 4,000 Jewish people.

Father Pierre-Marie Benoît (also known as Father Benedetto), lived in the Capuchin monastery in Rome when World War II began. Italy joined Germany and attacked France. Father Benoit, a French national, returned to the Capuchin monastery in Marseilles, France. France was defeated and the city of Marseille was governed by the fascist Vichy government. Like their Nazi friends in Germany, the government imposed Nazi racial laws and began arresting Jewish people. Father Benoit immediately opened his monastery and helped hundreds of Jewish people escape arrest and deportation. The Gestapo learned of his activities. To avoid arrest, Father Benoit returned to the Capuchin monastery in Rome and continued his rescue activities.

Soon after Father Benoit returned to Rome, the German army occupied the city. There were thousands of Jewish people in Rome. Many were Italians who had lived in Italy for centuries, others were refugees who had escaped from France, Yugoslavia and other countries. Escape routes were closed, and foreigners were immediately suspect. Father Benoit knew the Chief Rabbi of Rome and offered to help.

27

He began to work with DELASEM (*Delegazione Assistenza Emigranti Ebrei*) the Jewish rescue and relief organization in Italy.

Early in the morning of Oct. 16, 1943, the German police raided the Jewish neighborhood in Rome. A thousand Jewish men, women and children were rounded up and arrested. Soldiers and trucks blocked every entrance to the district. The president of DELASEM was arrested and Father Benoit was elected its new president. For the next nine months, Father Benoit worked ceaselessly to organize rescue activities.

The Gestapo was relentless in the hunt for Jews. Father Benoit knew it was time for DELASEM to go underground and asked his superiors for permission to move the office to the monastery. The Father Superior agreed and the headquarters of DELASEM was moved to the Monastery at 159 Via Silicia in the middle of Rome. As a pontifical college, it came under the protection of the church and soldiers were not allowed to come inside.

Gestapo headquarters were located across the street from the monastery and the Nazi officers could see the continual coming and going of strangers. But that did not stop Father Benoit. He told the younger priests, "There is nothing to fear. The monastery is protected by the church and I take all the responsibility." But no one suspected that there would be so many people seeking help.

Every day, more refugees came seeking help. Men, women, and children, homeless and frightened came to the monastery. They were told to come to the side entrance.

Father Benoit took care to meet and talk with every refugee. He made everyone feel welcome and offered comfort as well as help. Little children often sat in his lap while he talked with their parents. Father Benoit spent many hours talking and arranging hiding places for everyone who sought his help. When a group of people were hidden in an orphanage, it was Father Benoit who came to warn them that they needed to move. The Germans were in full control of the city, everywhere people were being stopped and questioned and asked to show their identification papers. The refugees had no identification papers.

Italian Jews needed safe places to hide, but refugees from other countries needed more help. They were conspicuous. Most of them did not speak Italian and had no means of support. They not only had to be hidden, but they had to be hidden where they could not be seen. Funds for food, clothing and medicine had to be distributed, identification papers and ration cards had to be obtained.

The funds for food and clothing were supplied by DELASEM. Together with other members of the relief organization, Father Benoit built a secret network. He found safe hiding places in private homes, monasteries, convents and churches and arranged to get false baptismal certificates.

Father Benoit knew that a sudden flood of baptismal papers would arouse suspicion and he sought the advice of an Italian policeman he trusted. Forged or stolen documents could not be used without raising suspicion. . The police officer advised him to get ration cards.   With hundreds of refugees safely hidden, Father Benoit found an old printing press in the monastery basement and arranged to print false identification papers. He spoke to the British Ambassador to the Vatican and got his help in obtaining documents for foreign Jews.

Although the work was dangerous, Father Benoit was confident that the hidden refugees were safe.

One afternoon two men claiming to be refugees came to the door. They were big tall men and looked well fed. They did not speak like other refugees.

Let us in. We are Jewish refugees, one man sad gruffly.

Father Benoit was immediately suspicious and did not invite them to come inside.

Why have you come here? he asked.

You know why we are here. You give shelter to Jews. We need shelter," one of the men said in a loud voice.

Why do you come here? Father Benoit spoke in a quiet voice.

The man was impatient and arrogant. "We are Jews and know you help Jews."

Father Benoit took a deep breath. "Oh, my friends. You are in the wrong place. What would we have to do with the Jews? We are poor monks who know nothing. I regret that I cannot help you. I will ask the fathers to pray for you," he told them and closed the door.

A few days later, Father Benoit found out that he was right to be suspicious. The men were Gestapo agents.

Father Benoit had not given much thought to the danger of his activities until the Gestapo came. The monastery was a pontifical college under papal supervision. This meant the Gestapo could not arrest anyone in the monastery unless they were caught in the act of rescue. Father Benoit was worried that a group of Jews would come seeking help at the same time the Gestapo was around.

DELASEM could no longer distribute clothing and food from one place. The distribution center had to be moved frequently. The clothing for the refugees was stored in convents.

DELASEM entrusted its funds to Cardinal Boetta in Genoa, who sent them by messengers to Father Benoit. In December, the Cardinal gave the money in cash to the messenger. On the way back to Rome, the messenger was arrested by the Gestapo. Father Benoit had no money to purchase supplies. He went to the American and British ambassadors at the Vatican who contacted the American Distribution Committee. The American group agreed to send money to London.

Mr. Osborne the British ambassador told him the money could not be transferred. He advised him to find people in Italy to advance the money and they would be repaid at a later date. Father Benoit spoke to people he trusted and found two generous people who were willing to advance the money. The Vatican got in touch with the American Catholic Distribution Refugee Committee and contributed funds.

With the money problem solved, Father Benoit turned his attention to the making of identification papers. He found an old printing press in the basement of the monastery and had it cleaned and oiled. With the help of friendly foreign diplomats, and a man skilled at the making of documents, hundreds of identification papers were produced. False names to be used on the documents and they had to look like other identification papers and have the necessary stamps and seals. Father Benoit inspected each one sand distributed them to the refugees.

The Gestapo were determined to trap Father Benoit and planned to raid the monastery. Someone from the Vatican warned Father Benoit just in time. It was 2 o'clock in the morning, he left the monastery by the side door just a few minutes before the raid and hurried to the convent of the

Capuchin Sisters and told them about the raid. The Mother Superior told him to come inside. He shaved his beard and dressed as a nun, he stayed at the convent for a week.

Piles of books in the basement hid the printing press. The Gestapo found nothing. The Allies were getting close to Rome, but the Gestapo kept searching. A warrant for Father Benoit's arrest was sent out. When they did not find anything at the Capuchin monastery, they raided another convent. Father Benoit managed to escape arrest.

The Allies entered Rome in June 1944 and the Germans fled the city. The people of Rome danced in the streets. They welcomed the American troops. The refugees came out of hiding and the synagogues were opened once again. Father Benoit ended his presidency of DELASEM, but he was honored and named honorary president for life.

A special ceremony was held in the largest synagogue of Rome to honor Father Benoit. The children wrote and sang a canticle. The men and women who were saved by Father Benoit, rose to pay tribute to him.

"My friends let us rise. Let us turn our eyes to Father Benoit and to his brethren. For us, these men are the personification of goodness, of love, of humanity, Let us thank them." (p. 161)

Father Pierre-Marie Benoit was honored by the Yad Vashem, the Holocaust Memorial Center in Israel, as one of "righteous" among the nations.

References:

Leboucher, Fernande (1969) *Incredible Mission* N.Y. Doubleday and Company.

Paldiel, Mordecai (1993) The Path of the Righteous: Gentile Rescuers of Jews during The Holocaust. Hoboken, N.J.: KTAV Publishing House.

Don Arrigo Beccari: A Safe Haven In Villa Emma

It was long train ride from Yugoslavia to Italy. No one knew what to expect. The children were good actors and hid their fear in silence. They were Jewish child refugees from Germany, Austria, and Poland, their parents had been deported to Nazi concentration camps. Josef Ithai, the young teacher who looked after them, shared their fear.

Ithai was only 23 years old when he took the children to Yugoslavia. They were on their way to the British mandate of Palestine, the land that was to become Israel. Two other adults accompanied them. When they arrived in Yugoslavia, the country was occupied by German and Italian troops. Travel to Palestine was not possible. Ithai and the children were in the city of Zagreb in the German zone and Jewish people were being arrested.

You see, Hitler is chasing us again and one day he'll catch us," one of the boys said to Ithai. The young teacher knew he was right, the children were in danger. He knew he had to get the children out of Zagreb as quickly as possible.

Bring them into the Italian zone, an Italian official told him. "We are Hitler's allies but we do not persecute Jews." The official arranged for Ithai to take the children to the province of Lubiana, in the Italian zone. The Italian Jewish relief organization gave Ithai money to rent an old castle, the Lesno Brdo. With the relief organization looking after them, the children moved into the old castle. Ithai was able to buy food and other necessities and he felt confident that the children were safe. They lived in the castle for one year, when the German troops took over the Italian zone. The children had to be moved, but where they go, where would they be safe? Ithai wondered.

You can take the children to Italy, a friendly Italian official told him. Arrangements were made and on July 18, 1942, the children were on their way to Italy. Ithai did not know how or where they would be living, he was told to take the train to Venice. Numb with fear, the older children held the hands of the young ones as they boarded the train.

Mario Finzi, the head of the Jewish relief organization met them at train station in Venice. He told Ithai that arrangements were made for the children to live in Nonantola, a small farming village north of the city of Bologna.

38

You'll be safe in Nonantola. With the help of the priests in the Abbey at Nonantola, arrangements have been made for the children to live in the Villa Emma, an empty mansion." Finzi explained that the Jewish Italian relief organization would pay all their expenses.

In Nonantola, you'll be able to set up a school program and the older boys and girls will be able to learn to farm. And after the war they'll be able to go to Palestine and live on a kibbutz (a farm cooperative program) ." Finzi shook Ithai's hand and took him to the train that would take them to Nonantola.

How could Mario Finzi be so sure, Ithai wondered. What would the villagers think about so many Jewish children coming to live in the small village? Only a few could speak Italian.

The young teacher's fears were quickly put to rest. As soon as the train came to a stop in Nonantola, they were met by a group of friendly villagers who came to welcome them. They gave candies to the children and walked with them to the Villa Emma.

The large mansion was empty, there was little furniture, no beds, chairs or tables. Women from the village brought food to the mansion and Father Arrigo Beccari came to greet them.

The tall priest in his priestly robe walked around the room shaking the children's hands. "You are safe now," he said. He could see the fear in their eyes and he wanted to reassure them.

Josef Ithai told Father Beccari. "They've suffered so much and they need so much," he explained.

They will not suffer any more, Father Beccari assured him. "You can be sure I'll do everything I can to help."

Ithai explained that he wanted to prepare the children to live in Palestine, he thought it was important that the children keep up with their studies and learn to farm and build furniture. Father Beccari was also a teacher and helped Ithai set up the school program.

Dr.Giuseppe Moreali, the village doctor, came to the Villa, introduce himself to Ithai and told him that if anyone became ill, Ithai was to call him.

The Jewish relief organization made the Villa Emma the headquarters of their organization. They supplied funds for food and other necessities and set up a warehouse at the Villa Emma. Within a short time, beds, tables and chairs, blankets and sheets were brought to the Villa. It took a only a few weeks to transform the deserted mansion into a real home.

Village women came to help the older girls cook. A village carpenter came and built a bathroom and showed the older boys how to make furniture. One room in the Villa was set up as a synagogue and with Father Beccari's help, the school program was organized and the children had school work to keep them busy.

Everyone felt safe and secure in Nonantola. The children sang songs, played games, went on picnics and hikes and even put on little shows to entertain the village people who came to visit them. There was always something to do at the Villa Emma. More children arrived, there were one hundred and four children living at the Villa Emma.

This situation is ideal and the children are adjusting very well. Some are even learning to speak Italian," Ithai told Father Beccari.

After just one year of the idyllic life at the Villa, Italy was defeated by the British and Americans. It was September 1943. No one in the village suspected that the German troops would take over northern Italy.

Father Beccari saw the German army come into Nonantola. A hospital for German soldiers was set up across the street from the Villa Emma. A Nazi flag flew over its roof. The Villa Emma was no longer safe.

Father Beccari was warned that the Germans planned to arrest all the Jews in Nonantola. Rushing to the Villa, he told Ithai to bring the children to the Abbey.

The children could not be kept together, there were too many of them. Father Beccari went into the village and the surrounding countryside, he went from door to door asking people to hide the children. There was no shortage of volunteers, most families were willing to help. Within a few hours all the older boys and girls were hidden in homes in the village. The seminary took in the youngest children. The Villa Emma was empty.

It was no longer safe for the children in Nonantola. German soldiers were patrolling the village and someone might report the hidden children.

"How will it be possible to save us now? " Ithai wondered. He knew the priests and the people hiding children were risking their lives. How much more could he ask of them? But he did not have to ask.

Together with Monsignor Pilati and Dr Moreali, an escape route to Switzerland was planned. Dr. Moreali obtained blank identification cards and Father Beccari filled them in with false names. Dr. Moreali signed the cards. Five weeks later, the children and young people were taken to the train station.

Dressed in the uniforms of Catholic school children, Father Beccari went with them to the train station. Josef Ithai shook Father's Beccari's hand, "How can I ever thank you enough?. You have saved our lives."

You do not need to thank me. All I want is for the children to be safe." Father Beccari watched the children board the train.

The Swiss border was north and east of Nonantola. They had to change trains in Milan. The train that would take them to the border town did not leave until early the next morning. German soldiers were patrolling the train station.

Ithai took the children to an underground public washroom. They spent the night huddled together on the washroom floor. No one was able to sleep. Early the next morning, they left the washroom and boarded the small train that took them through the mountainous country to the border town. Father Beccari arranged for a local priest to meet them at the train station. The priest told Ithai they would have to walk the rest of the way.

I know the path very well, just follow me, he said. Holding the hands of the small children, the older girls and boys followed Ithai and the priest up a steep alpine path until they came to the Tresa River, a small rapid alpine stream.

We're going to have to walk across this stream.. We'll all hold hands." Like a human chain, Ithai took the children across the stream.

A Swiss guard came to meet them. Ithai showed the guard the identification papers Dr. Moreali had prepared. The guard let them enter Switzerland. Dr. Moreali knew people in Switzerland and he arranged for the children to stay in Bex-Les-Bains, a small town, where they lived until the end of the war.

After the war, Ithai was able to bring them to the British mandate of Palestine that was to become the State of Israel.

The children of Villa Emma never forgot Father Beccari, Dr. Moreali or the people of Nonantola. They planted one hundred trees in honor of the people of Nonantola and told everyone about Father Beccari, Monsignor Pilati and Dr. Guiseppe Moreali.

In Haifa, Israel a park, the "Gan Nonantola," was created to honor the citizens of the village. At the ceremony, a sculpture by one of the "children," Tilla Offenberger, was unveiled. The plaque reads in Hebrew and Italian:

"In honor of the citizens who under the guidance of the parish priest Don Arrigo Beccari and Dr. Guiseppe Moreali, righteous among the nations, saved during the Holocaust of 1943, 107 Jewish orphaned children of Europe. With eternal gratitude, the children of the Villa Emma."

Father Beccari and Dr. Moreali were honored by the Yad Vashem, the Holocaust Memorial and documentation center in Israel for their heroic rescue work.

Today, the Villa Emma Foundation, launched by Nonantola's mayor, Stefano Vaccari, promotes peace and Holocaust education.

References:

Ithai, Josef, (1987) "The Children of Villa Emma" In Hertzer, Ivo (Ed.)) *The Italian Refuge: Rescue of Jews During The Holocaust* Washington, D.C.: The Catholic University of America Press.

Sister Alfonsa

There were Catholic Sisters in every country in Europe who rescued Jewish children from Nazi terror, but rescue activities were most dangerous in Poland, where . hiding Jewish people was a crime punishable by death. The Nazis occupied Poland in 1939 and immediately began the merciless persecution of Jewish people. Hundreds of Jewish children were left abandoned, starving and homeless after their parents had been arrested.

"No human heart can stand the pain the Nazis are inflicting on Jewish children. Their parents are murdered in front of their eyes. They have no place to go, how are they to survive if we do not help them?" Sister Alfonsa (born Eugenia Wasowska) appealed to her superiors to give her permission to rescue Jewish children. She was sent to the Catholic orphanage in Przemysl, a city in southeastern Poland to look after 13 Jewish children who were taken into a Catholic orphanage with 40 Catholic children.

Sister Alfonsa arrived at the orphanage to find the Jewish children isolated from the others. They all slept in one room and did not go to school with the other children. Sister Alfonsa knew her job would not be easy.

Fear of being discovered was a constant threat. The identities of the Jewish children had to be kept secret, even from the other children. Their names were changed, they had to learn Catholic prayers, when to kneel and to make the sign of the cross.

Sister Alfonsa was determined to make life as normal as possible for the children in her care. She saw their fear and understood their pain and knew how difficult it was for them to be given new names.

It was hard for adults to always be on guard, Sister Alfonsa thought, how much more difficult it is for children. Not only did the children lose their parents, they lost their identities. They were given different names and could not talk about being Jewish or where their homes were. Some of the children were very young. Sister Alfonsa felt their fear and confusion and decided to sleep in the same room with the children. At night she often held a weeping child in her arms.

.

Why does everyone hate Jews? One girl asked her.

Everyone does not hate Jews. Sister Alfonsa explained that the Nazis were cruel people. "They hate the

Poles too and are making us all suffer. But the war will end and we will all be free again" She encouraged the children to respect themselves and not forget their families or their religion.

How can we remember to be Jewish when we can't tell anyone?

You can tell me, she told them. But remember, we can only talk about Jewish things when we are by ourselves," she reminded them.

It's like we are living a lie, one of the girls remarked.

Sister Alfonsa agreed. "The Lord will forgive us, but He wants you to be safe." Her quick wit and constant vigilance provided the protection the children needed. One morning at breakfast, one of the boys grabbed a young Jewish boy by the arm and yelled at him, "You are a Jew, you shouldn't be here."

Sister Alfonsa went up to the boy, "Are you being a bully again?" she said and took the younger boy away.

During the day, Sister Alfonsa depended on the older children to look after the younger ones and kept them busy with school work and chores around the orphanage. To make sure that every child knew how to recite the Catholic prayers and when to make the sign of the cross, she taught them how to say the prayers. She wanted to be sure that everyone knew the prayers before she took them to church with the other children. It was easier to work with the smaller children who had few memories of their Jewish past, but the older children struggled with their identities. Some resisted learning the prayers.

I don't want to change my religion, one girl confide to her. "My father was a Rabbi and taught me wonderful things about Judaism.

And you must remember the teachings, Sister Alfonsa assured her and carefully explained that they had to learn the prayers not because she was trying to make them Catholics, but so nobody would suspect they were Jews.

We say different prayers, but we all pray to the same God," she reassured them.

Conditions were difficult, there was a shortage of food and supplies, but Sister Alfonsa gave them the help they needed. The children trusted her. Under her care they felt safe. She was like a mother to them.

After the Allies won the war and Poland was liberated, Sister Alfonsa took the 13 children to the Jewish Committee. "They are Jewish children and belong to the Jewish people," she said.

In 1980, Sister Alfonsa traveled to Israel to meet with six people who were among the children she had rescued.

Thirty-five years had passed, but they recognized her as soon as they saw her.

You did not forget me, she said.

We'll never forget you, one of the women said with tears in her eyes.

Sister Alfonsa, you blessed us and saved our lives during very difficult times. We all feel so privileged to know you," Miriam Klein, one of rescued children said.

"This is the happiest moment of my life," Sister Alfonsa replied. At a dinner in her honor, everyone had a story to tell about the young sister who protected them. A tree was planted in her honor at the Garden of the Righteous at the Yad Vashem Memorial in Israel. She was given a medal and honored with other Polish nuns.

No one knows exactly how many Jewish children were rescued by nuns in Poland. Few documents were kept for fear of discovery. The nuns in Poland sheltered Jewish people in convents, schools, orphanages, poorhouses, and children's hospitals. The cases that have been documented represent only a few of the heroic rescues that took place.

References

Kurek,Ewa, (1997) *Your Life Is Worth Mine: How Polish Nuns Saved Hundreds of Jewish Children in German-Occupied Poland, 1939-1945,* NY:Hippocrene Books Inc.

Zielinski, Father Zygmunt. "Nuns Who Saved Polish Jews." *National Catholic Register* (2000).

Rescue in Hungary: The Bravery of Sister Margit Slachta.

"I stand without compromise, on the foundation of Christian values; that is, I profess that love obliges us to accept natural laws for our fellow-men without exception, which God gave and which cannot be taken away."

Margit Slachta

Sister Margit Slachta , Mother Superior of the Social Sisters in Hungary, is credited with rescuing more than two thousand people. Born in Kassa, Hungary in 1884, Sister Margit was a champion of human rights and the first woman to be elected to the Hungarian Parliament un 1920. A pioneer in social services, Sister Margit established the Society of Social Service to help homeless and desperate women. Dressed in their gray habits, the Social Sisters went into the poor sections of Budapest, they opened soup kitchens and provided shelter to homeless women.

Between 1941 and 1945, Sister Margit was actively involved in the rescue of Jewish people. The more she learned about the savagery of the Nazis, the more action she took. Her courageous campaign against Nazi savagery began when Hungary became Germany's ally in World War II and enacted its first anti-Jewish laws.

"These laws are a violation of the rights of all people," Sister Margit declared and pleaded with church and government officials to oppose them. She traveled throughout Hungary to lecture on the evils of war and racism and spoke in more than 50 towns with as many as three to four thousand people in attendance. She wrote many articles in her newspaper, "The Voice of the Spirit."

Sister Margit wrote, "The cataclysm that now sweeps through the world will spare only the person, or the nation, that recognizes its own sins and repents, and with that repentance will weep with those who weep, shows compassion to those who suffer and on those whose souls shines with the Christian emblem."

The plight of homeless Jewish refugees who were trying to come to Hungary came to Sister Margit's attention. To see the conditions for herself, she traveled to the border countries. In Slovakia, she saw hundreds of starving and destitute people who were forced to live in a nearby forest under armed guards. Sister Margit gave money to a local priest to bring food to the camp and joined other church officials to demand that the government allow the refugees entry to Hungary.

The government relented and allowed the refugees to enter the country, but the victory was short-lived. A few months after they arrived, approximately 20,000 refugee Jews were rounded up and deported. Sister Margit once again pleaded with church officials to take action and flew to Rome to appeal to the Pope. Her efforts helped to persuade Slovakian bishops to speak out against the deportations.

After fourteen thousand Jewish refugees were brutally murdered by German soldiers and the Ukrainian militia, Sister Margit Sclachta went on a trip to the Ukraine with the papal nunciate, Imre Szabo. The desperate plight of the Jewish people hiding in the forests, shaped her resolve to take an even more active role in rescue.

When she returned to Hungary, she spoke with the other sisters and made everyone aware of the plight of persecuted Jews. The Sisters agreed to open the doors of their homes to shelter refugees. One of the first people to be hidden was Dr. Magda Gross, a Jewish physician. Sister Margit taught her how to conduct herself like a nun and put her to work in the work in the convalescent home for children next door to the mother house in Budapest. She also hid Jewish children in the home.

Sister Margit often went to the home to make sure the children were safe. One day a policeman came to the home and questioned the children. Sister Margit went up the officer and scolded him, "Do you think we are raising bulls here that you need to know their pedigree' The policeman did not argue with her and left.

German troops marched into Hungary in March 1944 and the fate of the Jews was sealed. . Conditions steadily worsened. Adolf Eichmann, an officer of the Nazi SS began the murderous campaign against the Jewish population of Hungary. Arrests, deportations, and transportation to death camps took place all over Hungary. In Budapest, their homes were confiscated and Jewish people were forced into designated apartment buildings. About 25,000 Jews from the suburbs of Budapest were rounded up and transported to the death camps. The Hungarian fascist Arrow Cross guard eagerly helped the German troops. "The Voice of the Spirit" Sister Margit's publication was declared to be illegal. She took it underground and printed it secretly and made no secret of her opposition to the Nazi actions. All Jewish people were isolated in ghettos at the edge of the city, there was little food, and no help. Sister Margit pleaded with a church official to help. .

The church official told her she was putting the Sisters in danger by being so outspoken.

"To whom can the Jews turn for 'merciful compassion' if not to the church?" she replied and made no secret of her disappointment in church officials who refused to take action.

The Germans are losing the war, but that does not stop them from murdering innocent people. We will not hide our faces from the eyes of God, and we will save as many people as we can." she told the other nuns.

Rescue work was extremely dangerous. The Social Sisters took off their gray habits and wore secular clothing so they would not be easily recognized. The sight of starving people crowded together in buildings marked with a Jewish star showed them the importance of their work. They brought food to more than 2,000 people a day.

On their way to the ghettoes, they saw people being taken out of the buildings and forced to march to the trains that would take them to the death camps. Everyday they were witness to ruthless killings by the fascist Hungarian Arrow Cross and Nazi troops. When the Germans ordered the houses to be evacuated, the Sisters went into the ghettoes to bring people out. Families were hidden in the convent and children were hidden in the convalescent hospital.

Sister Margit relied on Sister Sarah Salkahazi, to bring people out of the besieged buildings. Sister Sara was arrested by Hungarian Nazis as she was taking two young Jewish women to a hiding place. Taken to the Danube River, they were forced to line up and face the river. Before the shooting began, Sister Sarah turned around, faced her assailants and made the sign of the cross. The bodies of the women were thrown into the river. Sarah Salkahazi was only 44 years old.

Sister Margit refused to let the terror stop the activities of the Social Sisters .Every one of their houses in Budapest became secret sanctuaries for refugees and others who were fleeing from the Nazis. The Social Sisters saved over 2, 000 lives.

After World War II, Sister Margit Slachta immigrated to the United States and worked with the Sisters of Social

Service in Buffalo New York until her death in 1974. In America, she was known as Sister Margaret Schlachta.

References

Braham, Randolph L. (1994) *The Politics of Genocide: The Holocaust in Hungary,* vols. I & II, New York: Columbia University Press.

Paldiel. M. (1993) *The Path of the Righteous: Gentile Rescuers of Jews During The Holocaust,* Hoboken, New Jersey: KTAV Publishing House

Schmidt, Maria (1987)"Action of Margit Slachta to Rescue Slovakian Jews." Danubian   Historical Studies, 1,Vol/ : 58; G. Rocca, col. 1434 - 1435.

.

Refuge in the Ecole St. Francis and Escape To Switzerland

German troops stormed into the Italian zone in southeastern France on November 8, 1943 when Italy was defeated by the Allies. Under the Italian occupation, Jewish people were safe, but now they faced arrest and deportation to Auschwitz, the death camp. The only chance to escape from Nazi persecution was to go into hiding or escape into Switzerland.

Crossing the border into Switzerland was dangerous, escapees had to make their way through narrow, steep and rocky mountain paths and faced the constant danger of being caught and arrested by French or German border guards or turned away by Swiss guards. Jewish refugees needed identification papers and trustworthy guides to lead them across the border and once across, they needed to know where it was safe for them to live.

A network of dedicated priests in Lyon and other towns and villages close to the Swiss border helped hundreds of Jewish people escape. Forged identification papers were obtained and contact was made with people in Switzerland who were willing to help. Trustworthy escorts able to guide

61

people through the rough mountainous terrain also had to be found.

Abbe Simon Gallay played a leading role and established contact with people in Switzerland. He made sure that the guides who were chosen were trustworthy and knew the country well. To avoid suspicion, refugees traveled in small groups and carried little baggage.

Surrounded by alpine cliffs, the Ecole St. Francis, a Catholic seminary in the village of Ville Le Grande was situated next to the border between France and Switzerland. This made it an ideal departure point. The school's garden was at the edge of the barbed wire fence that separated France and Switzerland. Father Pierre Frontin, the head of the seminary, Brothers Louis Favre, Francois Favrat, Gilbert Pernoud, and Raymond Broccard, the school's gardener, welcomed refugees and escorted them across the border.

It was late in the afternoon, heavy rain splashed the windows of the seminary. Father Favre stood and the window looking for a group of refugees to arrive. They were expected earlier in the day. As soon as he saw the small group of people struggling up the steep path to the seminary, he went to the door to greet them. Gasping for breath with water dripping from their clothes, three women, an elderly man and a teen-aged boy came to the door.

Come inside quickly, I've been waiting for you, " " Father Favre greeted them.

"We had a narrow escape," the woman who was their guide explained. "A German soldier saw us walking up the path and started to come after us. We ran into the woods and stayed there until we were sure he was gone."

You've had a long hard walk, but you are safe now, my friends," Father Favre reassured them. Narrow escapes from German patrols were frequent.

Father Favre brought them towels and took them into the kitchen and sat with them at the table. While they ate, Father Favre talked with them. No stranger to stories of separated families, forced arrests, anguish and terror, Father Favre saw the terror in their eyes. .

The teen-aged boy told Father Favre that his family had been arrested, the two women were separated from their children who were hidden in another village, the elderly man was a Rabbi, his wife was murdered by a German soldier. Father Favre listened to their stories. The stories of people robbed of their families, their homes, their belongings, and their identities were all too familiar to him. In some groups there were children so frightened they could not speak. Father Favre said a silent prayer, he was grateful he had the chance to help them.

When there were children in the group, he gave them school uniforms and brought them into his classroom. "Your parents can come to my classroom too," he told them.

Everyone had questions about the escape route. German guards patrolled the border and walked around the wall of the seminary. The refugees had to stay at the Ecole and learn how to navigate the escape route. It was easy to make a wrong turn and get lost in the woods. Before an escape was attempted, Father Favre wanted to made sure that everyone knew every step of the escape route. He also made sure that everyone had the correct identification papers. .

Beds were prepared and the refugees spent the next few days learning about the escape route. Father Favre brought out a map of the route they were to follow and explained every step of the way. When he was sure everyone knew the path by heart, he felt ready to take the refugees to the border.

On the day of the escape, Father Favre gathered the small group together.

We have no more than two and a half minutes to leave the building and make our way to the path. The school's gardener will sit at his upstairs window watching the German guard. As soon as the guard turns around the garden wall, we will leave," he told them.

The gardener sat at the upstairs window waiting for the guard to turn around the wall, then he raised his hat as a signal. Everyone rushed to the door and made a run up the path to the border. Father Favre stood near the barbed wire fence as the Swiss guard checked their identification papers. After seeing that everyone was safely across the border, he came back to the seminary and waited for another group to arrive.

Sometimes people were refused and Father Favre brought them back to the seminary. After a few days, the gardener took them to the train station in Annemass, a nearby town, to try a different route.

In July, 1944, the Gestapo raided the seminary and arrested the priests. Father Favre was tortured and executed by the Gestapo, Father Frontin and the other priests were put in prison. The seminary was closed.

Survivors never forgot the courage and the kindness of the priests at the Ecole St. Francis. "We were always welcomed with open arms," they said. The priests of the Ecole St. Francis were honored by the Yad Vashem.

References

Paldiel, Mordecai, (1993) *The Path of the Righteous: Gentile Rescuers of Jews During the Holocaust..* Hoboken, N.J. KTAV Publishing House.

Zucotti, Susan (1993) The *Holocaust, the French and the Jews.* N.Y. : Basic Books, division of Harper Collins.

Father Adam Stzark

Father Adam Sztark, was pastor of the Jesuit church in Slonim, he was also the rector of the Marion Shrine and chaplain of the hospital. Slonim.is located on the banks of the Schara River and was part of Poland when it was occupied by the German army in 1941.(It is now under the jurisdiction of Belorussia).

As soon as the Germans occupied the city, anti-Jewish laws were enforced, Jewish people were robbed of their homes and belongings and forced to live in a small section of the city, known as the ghetto. A wooden wall surrounded the ghetto and was guarded by German soldiers.. At the beginning of the war, 213,000 people lived in Slonim, 21,000 were Jewish.

Father Sztark was on his way home from the hospital, it was early morning. He had been the hospital all night to comfort the family of a dying man. He heard cries and screams and saw the German soldiers pushing and shoving a group of women and children out of the ghetto.

A small boy ran out of the ghetto gate sobbing. "I want to be with my mother." A German soldier grabbed the boy. Father Stzark quickly stepped up to the soldier. "Leave the boy alone, " he said. .

What is a priest doing with the Jews" he sneered. "Don't you know you are not allowed to be here, You are not allowed to be in the ghetto," the soldier shouted.

I do not intend to go into the ghetto, but I'm not going to stand by while you hurt a small child," he said. The soldier shrugged and went back to the others. The women were taken away.

Father Sztark stayed with the little boy and took his hand.

My mother made me hide..she did not want me go with her," the boy sobbed.

Your mother wants you to be safe and I am going to keep you safe." Father Sztark told the boy. Under the eye of a German guard, Father Sztark took the boy out of the ghetto. As they walked through the silent streets, he wondered how many children there must be who are alone and abandoned and living under these cruel conditions." The Lord has given me a mission" he told himself. Determined to save as many children as he could. He brought the boy to the Convent of the Immaculate Conception. If he was to save children he needed the help of the nuns in his parish

Mother Superior Maria Woloska and and Sister Maria Ewa Noiszewska were in the parlor when Father Sztark came into the convent. With one look at the little boy, the Mother Superior asked one of the sisters to look after him. Father Sztark told them about what he had seen and how much he wanted to save children. .

He did not need to say any more to the Sisters. They knew immediately what needed to be done.

Of course we will help you, Father. Mother Maria told him. "We can hide children in the attic and look after them."

You realize that it will be very dangerous to hide Jewish children." Father Szrtark warned them Hiding Jewish people was a crime punishable by death under the Nazi occupation.

It is what the Lord wants us to do,". Father Sztark told himself and left the little boy to the convent. The nuns agreed to take in more children and Father Sztark returned to the ghetto. He found children living in the streets, their parents had been arrested and they had no where to go. Every time he went into the ghetto he found more children.

The nuns made the attic of the convent comfortable for the children. They managed to get a supply of food and clean clothing. . Soon the convent was full. Father Stzark placed some children with families who were willing to take them and kept children in the church. Many people in the parish were helping to supply food.

Father Sztark's frequent visits did not go unnoticed by the German guards. They followed his movements and watched the convent. Father Sztark knew he was under suspicion, but he was willing to take the risk.

In December, 1942, the Mother Superior and Sister Maria had just finished their morning prayers when they heard a loud knocking on the door. Before Mother Maria could open the door, she heard a crashing sound. Gestapo troops broke into the convent.

We know you are hiding Jews here," the chief officer shouted. Who is helping you?"

Mother Maria stood up. "This is a convent, Sir. How dare you crash in here."

Who is helping you take care of the Jews?" the Gestapo officer shouted again. Sister Maria came into the room and stood close to Mother Superior.

You will be punished unless you tell us who is helping you. "

The Mother Superior together with Sister Maria refused to betray the people who were helping them look after the children.

You had better cooperate or you will be severely punished." The Gestapo officer warned them before he left.

The Gestapo came back the next day. The nuns refused to betray the people who trusted them. The two nuns were taken to a nearby execution site, a place called Gorki Pantalowickie, where they were thrown into a pit and murdered.

Without warning, two days after Christmas the Gestapo officers arrested Father Sztark at his home in the Marion Shrine and ordered him to come with them.

Come just as you are. You cannot take anything with you." The Gestapo officer said.

I want to say Mass and will need to bring some bread," he told them.

The Gestapo officer pushed him out of the door. "Where you are going, there's plenty of bread!" the officer said in a merciless tone of voice.

Father Sztark knew he would be murdered just as the nuns had been a few days earlier. He was taken to same site and was ordered to undress.

I am prepared to die, but I will die in my black robe of the Jesuit order," he told his killers.. For some reason they granted him his last wish. With his last gasp, he managed to stand up, "All for Christ the King! Long Live Poland!" he gasped before he died. Father Sztark was thirty-five years old.

Farther Sztark, Mother Superior Maria Kowalska and

Sister Maria Ewa Noiszewska were honored by the Yad Vashem. Father Sztark is regarded as one of the distinguished martyrs of the twentieth century by the Catholic Church.

Reference:

Lapomarda, Rev. Vincent A. (1983) *Five Heroic Catholics of the Holocaust*. Jerusalem Israel: Yad Vashem Studies, vol 15. .

Resistance and Rescue: Father Pierre Chaillet (France)

France signed an armistice with the Germans on June 22, 1940. The country was divided into two zones: the "Occupied Zone" ruled by the Germans, included northern France and the Atlantic coast, the "Free Zone" in the south was ruled by a French collaborationist government that complied with Nazi anti-Jewish laws. Beginning in 1941, Jewish refugees fleeing from Nazi persecution were arrested by the French police and imprisoned in internment camps.

Father Pierre Chaillet (1900-72) , a Jesuit priest and teacher of theology joined other Catholic priests and Protestant pastors in the city of Lyon to establish a secret underground newspaper, the "Cahier du Temoignage Chretien" (Christian Witness) to resist the French government's collaboration with the Nazis. Father Chaillet wrote articles protesting the cruel persecution of Jews. The first issue was printed in 1941 and made a strong case for active resistance against persecution.

The church cannot disinterest itself in the fate of man, wherever his inviolable rights are unjustly threatened.

When one member (of the human race) suffers, the entire body suffers with him," Father Chaillet declared. With support from Cardinal Henri de Lubac and other Catholic and Protestant leaders, the newspaper was printed regularly and distributed to all the bishops in the southern section of France. Father Chaillet wrote about the roundups and arrests that were taking place in Paris. .

Thousands of Jewish refugees fled to the south of France and lived in horrible conditions in shelter camps. In 1941, Father Chaillet worked with Abbe Alexandre Glasberg 1902-81) and organized the "Amities Chretienne" (Christian Fiends) to coordinate rescue activities together with Jewish rescue groups. With the support of Cardinal Gerlier of Lyon, the committee provided false identity papers, ration cards, distributed food and offered aid to refugee Jews. Under the supervision of the Amities Committee, Catholic and Protestant social workers brought food and medicine into the camps. Special efforts were made to rescue children. The Committee rescued resistance fighters as well as Jewish people.

When the roundups and arrests of Jews began in Lyon in 1942, Father Chaillet became an active rescuer The Archbishop of Toulouse, Jules Gerard Saliege and Bishop

Pierre Theas of Montauban gave their support to the Committee. Archbishop Saliege encouraged the churches to open the doors of convents and monasteries.

In the early morning hours in August, 1942, the French police drove in black cars to every place in Lyon where Jews were in hiding and took them to an internment camp in Venissieux outside of Lyon.

Church leaders in Lyon and the surrounding area protested. Elderly and frail, Archbishop Saliege wrote a letter to all the parishes in his district.

It has been reserved to our time to witness the sad spectacle of children, of women, of fathers and mothers, being treated like a herd of beasts; to see members of the same family separated one from another and shipped away to an unknown destination....Jews are men, Jewesses are women....They cannot be mistreated at will....They are part of the human race. They are our brethren as much as are so many others. A Christian cannot forget that." The letter was distributed throughout the diocese on August 30. 1942.

Monsignor Pierre-Marie Theas', the archbishop of the neighboring city of Montauban wrote a similar letter to the parishes in Montauban.

I give voice to the outraged protest of Christian conscience, and I proclaim that all men, whether Aryan or non-Aryan, are brothers because they were created by the same God: and that all men, whatever their race or religion, have a right to respect from individuals and well as from States." The letter was also distributed and read on August 30, 1942.

Persecution continued, Jews were arrested and sent to a transit camp at Vennisieux, near Lyon to await deportation to Auschwitz, the death camp. The night before the Jews at the transit camp at Vennissieux were to be deported, Abbe Glasburg and Father Chaillet sent a group of social workers into the camp to rescue children and took them out of the camp. The French police went to Cardinal Gerlier to demand that the children be surrendered, but Cardinal Gerlier refused. The police arrested Father Chaillet and kept him imprisoned for three months. To avoid arrest. Abbe Glasburg escaped from Lyon.

Shelter camps were set up for the Jewish people who escaped arrest, but they were no longer safe, they had become booby traps. Children and adults had to be hidden in churches, monasteries and convents and with private families. Cardinal Gerlier encouraged churches, monasteries and convents to open their doors to Jewish children.

Hundreds of abandoned children, starving and desperate, were hiding in the tunnels and caves in and around Lyon. As soon as Father Chaillet was released in November, he devoted himself to the rescue of children.

Early every morning, dressed in his priestly robe, he roamed the narrow streets of Lyon and went into the tunnels beneath the hills Lyon looking for children. Searching the countryside, he found children living in caves in the mountains around Lyon. With the help of his parishioners, Father Chaillet found families willing to shelter children. People living in the villages around Lyon opened their doors to the children in response to Father Chaillet's pleas.

When German troops took over the unoccupied zone in November,1943, the search for Jews intensified. Klaus Barbie who was later called the "Butcher of Lyon" head of the Nazi Gestapo, was relentless in his search for Jews. In

January 1943, the Amities Committee called an emergency meeting to distribute false identification papers to the Jews in hiding. The Gestapo found out about the meeting and planned to raid the Committee offices. Germain Robiere, a young Catholic woman who worked with Father Chaillet, dressed as a cleaning woman and went to wash the floors of the office to warn the Jews to leave quickly. Escape into Switzerland was no longer possible and more hiding places had to be found for Jewish refugees.

In cooperation with Klaus Barbie, the French police continued to search for children, they arrested them and brought them to the police station. Father Chaillet went to the police station and demanded that the children be released to his care, he refused to leave until the children were released. His stubborn insistence persuaded a police captain to release the children to him.

Most of the homes that were set up to shelter abandoned children were closed as private homes were found for the children, but one home in the small village of Iziuex was still operating. It was thought to be safe because it was in a quiet village outside of Lyon. In April, 1944, the children in the home were eating breakfast when two trucks and two automobiles drove up to the house. Two German civilians and a group of German soldiers burst into the home and arrested the 44 children and the adults who looked after them. Forced into the trucks by the soldiers, the children were taken away. The only child who was released was not Jewish, all the others were taken to a death camp where they perished.

To avoid further arrests and betrayal, great care had to be taken to protect the children. Father Chaillet visited the homes where he placed children to make sure they were safe. Until the very end of the war, he continued to search for and rescue both children and adults.

Father Chaillet, Father Glasberg, Germain Ribiere have been honored by the Yad Vashem for their heroic rescue activities.

References:

De Lubac, Henri (1988) *Christian Resistance to Antisemitism: Memories from 1940-1944*. .San Francisco, California: Ignatius Press.

Klarsfeld, Serge (1984*) The Children of Izieu: A Human Tragedy*. NY: Harry N. Abrams

The Daring Rescue At the Tres-Saint-Saveur Convent (Belgium)

In the summer of 1942, the Nazi military police in Belgium were arresting and deporting Jewish people to the death camps. Cardinal Van Roey, Archbishop of Malines, strongly opposed the Nazis and assisted the Belgian secret Jewish rescue organization , the Comite' des Defense des Juifs (CDJ) to rescue people. Convents and monasteries under his jurisdiction opened their doors to hide Jewish children. Older women were given refuge in an old age home. In protest against Nazi racial laws and persecution, Cardinal Van Roey also told his priests to refuse to give communion to German soldiers in uniform or to Belgians who cooperated with the Nazis.

Sister Marie Amalie, the Mother Superior of the Tres- Saint- Saveur convent in Brussels quickly responded to the Cardinal's request. Fifteen Jewish girls ranging in age from seven and fifteen years of age girls were brought to the convent. For nine months, the nuns looked after them and made them feel safe. No one suspected that the Nazi Gestapo knew that Jewish children were being hidden in the convent.

It was a sunny spring morning on May 20, 1943. The girls were eating breakfast when Sister Marie heard the loud knocking on the door. Three Gestapo officers stood outside. As soon as Sister Marie opened the door, one of the officers shouted at her.

We know you are hiding Jewish girls. We have come to take them."

"I cannot let you take them away, " Sister Marie protested in a quiet voice. " They are innocent young children"

You know it is against the law to hide Jews, the officer scolded. If you don't give them to us, we will arrest you too."

Sister Marie looked into the officer's cold eyes and tried to hide her fear, "Then I suppose we have no choice but to give them to you. But you'll have to come back at another time. You see, most of the girls are not here now," she said in a firm but quiet voice.

"We'll be back tomorrow morning, but you better make sure all the girls are here,." the officer warned her.

Something had to be done to protect the girls. As soon as the Gestapo officers left, Sister Marie said a silent prayer and quickly made contact with Cardinal Roey and appealed to him for help. She also remembered the woman from the Jewish rescue organization who brought the girls to the convent and made contact with her.

The woman reassured her and told her that a rescue would be planned. "Help will be coming, but I cannot tell you anything more, " the woman told her. "Just make sure that the children are ready to leave tonight."

Sister Marie wanted to know more, but the woman could not tell her any details. Sister Marie had no idea how a rescue would be accomplished, she did not know that Paul Halter, a Jewish commander in the Belgian armed resistance had found out about the Gestapo's visit to the convent and was planning to rescue the girls.

"All we can do now is get the children ready to leave and pray," she told the other nuns.

By mid-afternoon, the girls had packed their few belongings. Girls who loved to chatter and play games, sat around in silence.

85

By nighttime, Sister Marie was worried. Where were the rescuers?, she wondered. She suspected that the rescue would take place in the dark, but it was getting past the curfew and no one had come. The hours passed slowly. The girls went to their beds fully clothed.

Just before 10 PM, the doorbell rang. Dressed in Nazi uniforms, two armed men forced their way into the convent shouting, "Hands up!" shouted Paul Halter. A member of the Belgian resistance, he took charge of the rescue. Two armed men and a woman, dressed in Nazi uniforms came with him.. They ordered Sister Marie and the other nuns to go to her office. They cut the phone lines and tied the other nuns to their chairs. Sister Marie did not protest, she knew they were the rescuers and were protecting the sisters by tying them up and locking the office door so the Gestapo would not think that they knew about the rescue operation.

It took less than an hour to get the girls out of the convent. Sister Marie could hear the girls crying. On the way out, to reassure the children, one of the men whispered a few words in Yiddish, a language many Jewish people spoke, to let the girls know they were they were safe.

Sister Marie calmed the other nuns and told them the children were being rescued. After the "kidnapping" the sisters waited before they called for help, they wanted to give the kidnappers time to get the girls to a safe place. After half an hour passed, one of the nuns managed to reach the window and shout to a passer-by to call the Belgian police. When the police came, the nuns told them the girls were kidnapped.

Cardinal Van Roey knew the details of the rescue and rushed to the convent. He insisted that the police wait until morning before speaking with the Gestapo. He wanted to make sure the rescuers had enough time to take the children in a safe place. Some were hidden in the homes of the rescuers.

The next morning, the Gestapo officers came to the convent to arrest the girls.

Officer, didn't you know that the Gestapo took the children away last night. The girls are not here."

The Gestapo officer accused her of arranging their escape.

They didn't escape, they were kidnapped," she insisted. " We thought they were being taken by the Gestapo."

"You would not let us take them yesterday, but you let the kidnappers take them," the officer said. .

"There was nothing we could do. We were locked up in the office. I was certain the men were sent by the Gestapo," Sister Marie repeated.. "They looked just like German soldiers."

"You just let them take the girls away without screaming," the officer looked at her coldly.

Scream? We didn't dare; they said they would shoot us if we made noise."

I do not believe you. If I find out you are lying, you will be arrested," he warned Sister Marie.

As soon as the Gestapo officer left, Sister Marie told the other nuns, "Our prayers have been answered. She explained that the rescue was arranged by Jewish leaders in the Belgian resistance who were helped by other resistance fighters. The girls were hidden in the homes of the resistance fighters. Soon after the war, Sisterr Marie found out that all fifteen girls survived.

Paul Halter, Toby Cymberknopf, and Bernard Fenerberg, Jankiel Parancevitch, Andrée Ermel and Floris Desmedt were the rescuers. Sister Marie Amilie and Cardinal Van Roey have been honored by the Yad Vashem.

Reference:

Paldiel, Mordecai (2003) "Abducted From the Hands of the Aggressor: The Rescue of Jewish Children in Belgium," Yad Vashem Quarterly Magazine, Vol 30, p. 5.

Sister Anna Borkowska, Lithuania

German troops were killing Jewish people in the forest outside of the city of Vilna in Lithuania. Sister Anna Borkowska, the Mother Superior of a small Benedictine convent and the seven sisters who worked with her, heard the screams and the gunfire. The Sisters refused to sit by and do nothing.

A graduate of Cracow University in Poland, Sister Anna moved to Vilna to take charge of the convent. When she arrived in Vilna, she was impressed by the beauty of the city with its beautiful churches and synagogues. With a population of two hundred thousand people, a third of them Jewish, Vilna was a vibrant city and a center of Jewish life. A beautiful synagogue was close to the convent. The peacefulness of the city came to an abrupt halt in 1941 with the arrival of German troops. In the midst of the battle between the Russians and the Germans, Vilna became a battleground.

The Germans immediately enforced their racial laws and forced the Jews to leave their homes and move to an old part of the city that has once been the Jewish ghetto. Thirty thousand people were moved into the six tiny streets of the ghetto. Robbing people of their belongings and forcing them to live in poverty was not enough for the Nazis. The ghetto was raided frequently and people were arrested. Young men and women were forced to work for the Germans.

Sister Anna knew what was happening in the ghetto. The convent was located near the ghetto. Sister Anna brought food and medicine to the ghetto and made contact with a Jewish rescue organization. Together, the sisters in the convent were prepared to rescue people and make the convent a place of refuge.

Abba Kovner, a young artist who was a leader of a group of young people who were determined to resist the Nazis met Sister Anna in the ghetto. Kovner wanted to organize a group of Jewish resistance fighters. .

Hitler is planning to kill every Jewish person. But we will not go as sheep to the slaughter. We have few weapons, but we are determined to fight." He told the Mother Superior.

Sister Anna invited him to bring a group of young people to the convent. "You will be safer in the convent and free to make your plans. We will help you, " she told Kovner.

The next day, Abba Kovner and sixteen other young people came to the convent.

Sister Anna welcomed them. Wearing the habits she gave them, the young men and women worked in the fields with the Sisters and made plans for organizing a resistance movement in the evening. Living outside of the ghetto gave Kovner the chance to meet with people who lived outside of the ghetto.

You are fighting a holy war, Sister Anna encouraged him. .

You are more than a friend, Kovner told Sister Anna. You are being a real mother to us. The young people called the Mother Superior, "Ima" (" mother" in Hebrew). She sat with them at their meetings and encouraged them to act. She wanted to be part of the group.

Kovner made contacts with people inside and outside of the ghetto who wanted to help and the United Partisans Organization was born.

Kovner told Sister Anna that it was time for him to leave. "I can't live in safety when my people are perishing, "

Kovner told Sister Anna and left the convent. He went back to the ghetto to recruit more people for the Partisans.

Sister Anna visited him and spent several nights sleeping in the squalor of the ghetto. "I want to fight by your side, " she said.

It's too dangerous for you to stay here. I'm afraid for you, Mother, Kovner told her. " You will be a bigger help to us on the outside. Here we are so isolated that we need you to keep open every link to the free world."

Sister Anna knew Kovner was right and went back to the convent.

.Every day more people were arrested, many were taken and murdered in the forest. The Sisters devoted themselves to hiding more people. The Germans planned clear the ghetto. One hundred young people joined the partisans and the fighting began. .

Wearing a tattered coat with a Jewish star, Sister Anna came to the ghetto with weapons hidden in her pockets.

It's too dangerous for you to come, Kovner told her. You risk your life every time you come here."

Sister Anna reached into her pocket and took out three pear shaped hand grenades and explained how they worked. I will get other weapons too, " she told him.

Kovner gathered the weapons, trained the new recruits and prepared for combat.

Sister Anna continued to search the countryside for weapons and brought them to the Partisans.

In September, 1943, German troops came into the ghetto. The Partisans escaped into the forest and fought until the end of the war. Sister Anna managed to keep contact with him and came under suspicion.

Close to the end of the war, a German army officer came to the convent and arrested Sister Anna. A few months later, the Germans lost the war and Sister Anna returned to the convent..

After the war, when Sister Anna was asked why she and the other Sisters were willing to risk their lives. She said, "It was our duty. I felt as if I were indeed their mother. . I only feel sad that I could not do more. I am also thankful to my superior in the Vilna Archdiocese, who gave us his support".

Abba Kovner made sure that Sister Anna was recognized for her heroism.

Sister Anna Borkowska was awarded a medal from the Yad Vashem and a tree was planted in her honor.

References:

Levin, Dov (1985) *Fighting Back: Lithuanian Jewry's Armed Resistance to the Nazis 1941-1945*. N.Y. Holmes and Meyer.

Paldiel, Mordecai (1993) *The Path of the Righteous: Gentile Rescuers of Jews During the Holocaust*. Hoboken, N.J.: KTAV Publishing House.

Cohen, Rich (2000) "The Avengers" . N.Y. Vintage Books (division of Random House.

Father Joseph Andre: Rescue In Belgium

When Belgium was occupied by the German army in 1940, there were 100,000 Jews living in Belgium, 20,000 were refugees from Germany. Arrests and deportations to the death camps began in 1942. . The Belgian Committee of the Defense of Jews (CDJ), a secret Jewish rescue organization, worked with the Belgian resistance. The Catholic church in Belgium under the leadership of Cardinal Van Roey encouraged priests and nuns to cooperate with the CDJ and hide people in monasteries, convents, and schools. Hundreds of Jewish children were rescued with the help of churches in every major city in Belgium.

Father Joseph Andre was the Abbey of the St. Jean the Baptiste church in Namur, a beautiful city on the Meuse River in the southern part of Belgium. When the German army occupied Namur and began to arrest and deport Jewish people, Father Andre went to the CDJ Committee to offer his help. "The doors of my church will always be open," he told them. A deeply religious man and a religious scholar, Father Andre had no idea how much his life was about to change.

A few days later Father Andre opened the doors of his church to a group of homeless children and quickly ushered them inside the church. He had never seen such terrified expressions on the faces of children and wanted them to feel welcome and safe. Living in alleys, starving and desperate, the relief organization sent them to Father Andre.

After welcoming them, he told them "This is your home now. My home is your home.".

One small boy gave Father Andre a letter from his mother.

Dear Father,

I do not know you, but I trust you to look after my son. He is only six years old and has never been away from home. I am heartbroken without him, but I want him to be safe. He is a good boy. Sometimes he might be mischievous but he means no harm. I am so very grateful."

Sincerely,

Aaron's mother

Father Andre had tears in his eyes as he read the letter. "Perhaps I can found out where your mother is and we could visit her together," he told the boy.

After a warm dinner prepared by the nuns, Father Andre talked with the children. He learned all their names and wanted to know about their families and their experiences.

It's bad to be Jewish. one little boy confided.

Father Andre comforted him. "We are all God's children. It is the Nazis who are bad, not the Jewish people. We are all the children of God."

Every week, more children came to the church. Father Andre spent his days searching for suitable homes. He went into the city and the surrounding countryside looking for people willing to take children. Father Andre traveled to nearby villages and searched the countryside looking for families willing to take a child. Older children could be more independent and could work on farms, but young children needed more care. Until Father Andre found a suitable home, he kept the children in the church.

The headquarters of the German army was directly across the street from the church. Keeping children in the church was dangerous, it was inevitable that the Germans would see children coming to the church. Without the help of his parishioners and neighbors, Father Andre knew he could not keep the children safe.

"Those Nazis won't give up until they murder every child," Father Andre told his neighbors. The doctor who lived next door to the church helped Father Andre build a camouflaged wall to hide the side entrance to his home to provide an escape route when and if German soldiers came to the church. Always on guard, Father Andre slept in a chair in his office.

When a family offered to take a child, Father Andre brought the child to the new home and often came to visit . He tried hard to meet the needs of the children in hi care. Every week he brought one little girl to visit her mother, who was hiding in another village. When one little boy became ill, he took him to the hospital under a false name. If any child was unhappy or neglected, he brought them to another place. And there were always children hidden in the church.

Father Andre did not let the children forget their Jewish heritage. He told them stories from the Bible. On the Passover holiday, the nuns to prepared a traditional Passover dinner, a seder. The holiday commemorates the miraculous escape from slavery in Egypt.

And we will know freedom again too, he reassured them.

The danger of a German raid was constant. Late one night, a loud knock on the door woke Father Andre. He jumped up from his chair and quickly woke the children up and took them through the camouflaged wall to the doctor's home. Then he came back and opened the door. The German Gestapo came inside and search the church.

We know you hide Jews, one of them sneered.

As you can see, there's no one here but me.

The soldiers walked through the church, "We'll be back, " the Gestapo officer said. "Everyone knows you are hiding Jews."

The raids became more frequent and Father Andre was threatened with arrest. He went into hiding and stayed away from the church until the liberation of Namur by the US

101

Army in 1944. After the German defeat, Father Andre brought the Jewish chaplain of the American army to the church to lead the children in prayer.

God is universal and we are all brothers, Father Andre told them.

After the war, Father Andre helped the children look for their parents. The orphans stayed at the church until October, 1945, when they were taken to a Jewish organization.

We will never forget you, the children told him. With tears in his eyes, Father Andre embraced each one and wished them well..

In 1967, Father Andre visited Israel to be honored. He met with many of the children he saved. Everyone had a story to tell of his bravery and his kindness, A tree in his honor was planted in the Garden of the Righteous at the Yad Vashem.

Gilbert, Martin. *The Righteous: The Unsung Heroes of the Holocaust* Toronto, Ontario: Key Porter Books.

Paldiel, Modecai., (1993) *The Path of the Rightwous: Gentile Rescuers Durng the Holocaust.* Hoboken, N.J. KTAV Publishing House.

Rescue in Rome

On October 16, 1943, Nazi troops surrounded the Jewish quarter in Rome and captured men, women and children, they dragged people from their homes, forced them into trucks and plundered the synagogue. More than a thousand people were arrested.

Rome was occupied by the German army in September, Nazi racial laws were immediately enforced, but no one imagined the horror that was to take place one month later. German troops were everywhere. With guns in their hands, they broke into the homes and shops of Jewish people. Many people left their homes and were taken in by neighbors, but hundreds were homeless and had nowhere to go.

When Pope Pius XII was told of the arrests, he took action and encouraged monasteries and convents to open their doors to Jewish people. Many priests and nuns responded. Of the 5,730 Jews who lived in Rome, 4, 238 found sanctuary in the monasteries and convents, 477 were sheltered in the Vatican and its enclaves.

Father Pietro Palazzini and Monsignor Roberto Ronca opened the doors of the Basilica of St. John Lateran, the oldest church in Rome. The massive white pillars in the front of the church became a beacon of hope for hundreds of Jewish refugees.

Working with Monsignor Roberto Ronca, Father Palazzini took in hundreds of refugees and arranged for people to be hidden in other monasteries and convents of Rome. Those who stayed at St. John Lateran were given jobs in the church library and in the church offices.

Danger was constant. Father Palazzini was well aware of the risk he was taking, the church could be raided at any time. Father Palazzini gave priestly robes to those who were able to work at the Basilica and kept everyone else carefully hidden. Although food was scarce, the nuns managed to prepare meals for everyone living at the church.

A nearby convent that was home to 60 orphans was raided, the sisters brought the orphans to the Basilica where they lived until Rome was liberated.

The convent on Via Caboto belonged to the Religious Teachers of Filippini was in the district. From the windows of the convent at Via Caboto, the sisters saw helpless people dragged from their homes and crowded into trucks. The Mother Superior, Sister Maria Pucci got permission from the Pope to open the three convents of the Fillipini Sisters to Jewish people.

Sister Maria Pucci described the first day of rescue, "It was very cold. We gave them what they needed, especially blankets to keep warm, Children were crying, hugging their mothers. They suffered terribly."

During the day, the Sisters Filippini taught their classes, at night they took turns staying up at night to guard them. During air raids, the refugees hid with the sisters in the basement of the convent. "We were all frightened. We prayed together. Prayers were mixed with tears. "

When asked why the sisters were willing to take the risk of hiding so many refugees, Sister Maria Pucci replied, "These people were our neighbors. We respected and loved them. We responded to the Pope's plea to open our doors."

After the war, a group of Jewish women made a gift of love to the Sisters of Filippini and presented with a five foot statue of the Madonna.

Twelve convents in Rome sheltered 1223 Jewish refugees. The Sisters of Our Lady of Sion hid 187 refugees Because it was outside of the Vatican's jurisdiction, the convent could be raided. The Mother Superior installed an alarm bell to warn the guests to hide when German soldiers came near the church. Refugees were also hidden in the Vatican itself and at the Pope's summer home in San Gandolfo. The priests and nuns who worked in the Vatican arranged for truckloads of food and clothing to be sent to all the convents and churches where refugees were hidden.

Monsignor Hugh O'Flaherty, an Irish priest who worked in the Vatican, played a major role in rescue operations of the Vatican and saved hundreds of people including Allied soldiers. . In full view of the German soldiers who were stationed outside of St. Peter's Square, Father O'Flaherty stood on the steps of St. Peter's church waiting for refugees to arrive and personally escorted them to the hiding places.

A tall athletic man, Father O'Flaherty was fearless and often left the Vatican to visit the soldiers and refugees. His movements were watched by Herbert Kappler, the head of the SS, who was determined to arrest him. Father O'Flaherty was told to hide and went to stay in the palace of Prince

Filipo Doria Pamphili. A few days later, SS troops raided the palace. Father O'Flaherty ran down the narrow stone staircase into the cellar, climbed up a pile of coal. When he opened the trap door to climb out, he saw that the SS troops were still there. Impatient , he decided to make an escape and disguised himself by taking off his black monsignor's robe and rubbing coal dust over himself. Then he calmly strolled past the two lines of SS troops and went into a nearby church to clean up before going back to the Vatican.

Father O'Flaherty continued his rescue operations and saved more Allied lives than any other single person in World War II.. His efforts earned him the nickname, "the Scarlet Pimpernel of the Vatican"

Many tributes were paid to Pope Pius XII for the rescue and shelter given to so many Jewish refugees. Rabbis, heads of Jewish organizations and survivors themselves expressed their gratitude to the Pope. The Congress of the Italian Jewish communities met in Rome in April, 1946 and paid expressed their "profound gratitude to him for helping Jewish people when their lives were endangered by Nazi-Fascist barbarism."

References:

Gallagher, J.P. (1967) *The Scarlet Pimpernel of the Vatican* N.Y,: Coward-McCann Inc.

Lapide, P. (1967) *Three Popes and The Jews: Pope Pius XII Did Not Remain Silent.* New York: Hawthorn Books. .

Marchione, Sister Margharita (1997) *Yours Is a Precious Witness: Memoirs of Jews and Catholics in Wartime Italy.* N.Y:. Paulist Press.

Rychlak, R.J. (2000) *Hitler, The War And the Pope.* Columbus, Missouri: Genesis Press.

More Heroes

There were many priests and nuns who rescued Jewish people. Some worked with the underground resistance movement and with Jewish rescue organizations. Many acted alone. This book would not complete without acknowledging the contributions of these heroic people.

Father Bernard Lichtenberg (1875-1943) was the priest of St. Hedwig's Cathedral, the largest Catholic church in Berlin, Germany. His many years of work among the poor led to his firm belief in the importance of defending and honoring all people, prompted him to protest Nazi racial laws and the cruel treatment of people with disabilities. To Father Lichtenberg, Nazi policies were an assault on religious beliefs. Assigned to St. Hedwig's Cathedral when the Nazis came to power, Father Lichtenberg reached out to help all persecuted people and ended his Sunday sermons with a prayer for Jewish people.

His public protests did not go unnoticed by the Gestapo who tried to silence him. Father Lichtenberg made no concessions and continued his crusade for the rights of all people. People warned him that he was in danger of arrest, but Father Lichtenberg refused to back down. In 1941, he was arrested by the Nazi Gestapo and was kept in prison for two years. . After his release, Father Lichtenberg went back to the church and continued to publicly pray for Jewish people. In 1943, he was arrested again. He died in the cattle car that was taking him to the concentration camp in Dachau.

Deeply loved and respected, four thousand people came to his funeral at St. Hedwig's church to honor him. In 1996, Father Lichtenberg was beatified by the Pope .

Cardinal Pietro Boetto (1871-1946), head of the Jesuit College in Genoa, Italy, was actively involved in the government of the Jesuit Order. Father Boetto worked with the Jewish rescue organization DELASEM ("Delegazione Assistenza Emigranti Ebrei.") and enabled hundreds of Jewish refugees to be hidden in the convents, rectories, and monasteries. Food, shelter, and false documents were given to the refugees and many were helped to escape into Switzerland. Cardinals Elia Dalla Costa of Florence, Ildefonso Schuster of Milan and Muarilio Fossati, Don Repetto and Don Giacomo worked with Cardinal Boetto. When the German army occupied northern Italy, escape was no longer possible, Cardinal Boetto continued to arrange hiding places for hundreds of Jewish people. He saved the lives of at least 800 people.

Father Jacques de Jesus (Lucien Burel, 1900-1945), a Carmelite friar, was headmaster of a school in Avon, France. Father Jacques hid young Jewish men and helped them avoid being sent to Germany as slave laborers. He hid Jewish children in his school, Petit College, Saint -Theresa de l'enfant Jesus and in the Convent des Carmes in Avon.. Father Jacques was arrested by the Nazi Gestapo and sent to a concentration camp where he was badly mistreated. He died soon after the camp was liberated by American troops. The world-famous French film-maker Louis Malle was saved by Father Jacques who paid tribute to him in his award winning film "Au Revoirs Les Enfants."

It is estimated that several thousand Jewish children were hidden in monasteries and convents in France. Reverend Father Superior Charles Devaux, director of Our Lady Zion and Mother Marie of Notre Dame de Sion-in Melen- hid 800 children in convents. Mother Marie-Angelique, Mother Superior of the Sisters of St. Joseph, arranged and supervised hiding Jewish children and members of the French resistance.

The Archbishop of Nice, Monsignor Paul Remond hid Jewish children in convents until they could be placed with families. Abbe Joseph Folliet, Catholic chaplain of the

113

Jeunesse Ouvriere Chretienne (JOC) arranged for Jewish refugees to stay at church sanctuaries in the department of Haute-Savoie. Bishop Gabriel Pignet arranged for Jewish children to be hidden in Sainte Marguerite, a Catholic boarding school and was arrested for his activities. Abbe Rene de Naurois of Marseille hid Jewish people with private families and Catholic institutions. After he joined the French resistance in 1941, he helped many Jews escape to Spain. Abbe Albert Gau, lived close to the Spanish border and helped many people escape.

Abbe Pierre Mopty traveled around the countryside searching for abandoned Jewish children and rescued them from a nearby French internment camp and took them in a canoe across the Lake Geneva to the Swiss side of the lake.

In Belgium, Father Bruno Reynder (1903-1981), a Benedictine monk, placed Jewish children in convents, secular institutions, and with private families throughout the Liege region of Belgium. . In addition to insuring the children's safety, Father Bruno provided the host families with food ration cards, false identities as well as financial aid. The Mont Cesar monastery near Louvain became the center of his rescue activities. Working with the JDC, the secret Jewish rescue organization, Father Bruno arranged the escape

114

of many Jewish refugees. Using his brother's house as a transit point, Father Bruno supplied ration cards, identification papers and financial support.

In April, 1943, Father Bruno was warned that the Nazi Gestapo was planning to raid his office in the monastery and arrest him. Father Bruno went into hiding. Discarding his monk's habit, he continued to rescue children and support them. . Father Bruno traveled between Louvain and Brussels and organized rescues under the eyes of the Gestapo. He even hid Jewish people in his own home.

When some of the host families requested his permission to convert the children in their care, Father Bruno responded: "We are responsible for the lives of these children, but their souls do not belong to us." One JDC executive emphasized that Father Bruno personally made all payments for the children in his care. Years later, when he visited Israel to plant a tree at Yad Vashem, Father Bruno recalled his war-time rescue activities: "Three hundred and sixteen Jewish souls passed through my hands, among them 200 children. I can't begin to tell you how many doors I knocked on. I literally wore myself out, but it was all worth it."

Every child he rescued, survived. After the war a ceremony was held at a synagogue to honour Father Bruno. The children gathered around him and pressed his arms while the parents, in tears, covered him with words of thanks and blessings."

A memorial dedicated to Father Bruno in Ottignies, Belgium reads, "Father Bruno Reynders, Benedictine Monk Hero of the Resistance. At the risk of his life saved some 400 Jews from Nazi barbarism."

Jewish children were also rescued by the Benedictine Sisters in Louvain who ran an orphanage. Sister Marie Leruth hid Jewish children at the La Providence orphanage in Verviers, near Antwerp and made sure they were safe. The Nazi Gestapo suspected that Jewish children were being hidden in the orphanage and began to visit the orphanage. Once, when a Nazi raid was expected, Sister Marie put the children put on a bus and took them to an outing to a nearby village for the afternoon. The children at the orphanage, described Sister Marie as "a marvel of love under circumstances which obliged her to risk her life and liberty every day."

A Benedectine orphanage in Louvain also hid many Jewish children. Rose Meerhoff, of Brussels, was seven years old in September, 1940, when her mother was arrested. A took her to the orphanage in Louvain, where she was welcomed by the nuns. Rose Meyerhoff later wrote, "I stayed in that convent for two and a half years, and I still have a special feeling for Catholics and nuns in particular. They were risking their lives for us."

Father Jakab Raille of the Jesuit College College in Hungary saved almost 150 people by hiding them in the Jesuit residence in Budapest. Brother Albert Pfleger, a French born monk of the Marist order also saved people during the German occupation of Hungary. Jews fleeing from the pro-Nazi Arrow Cross and Eichmann's SS squads were hidden in the monastery. Monsignior Angelo Rotto, the Vatican's ambassador to Hungary worked with other diplomats to stop deportations to death camps.

If God gave people life, no mortal man should be allowed to take it away or deprive them of a means of existence". Monsignor Rotto declared. He issued thousands of protective letters (19,000) and stayed in Budapest until the safety of the Jews in protective houses had been assured with the capture of Budapest by Russian troops.

Father Stakauskas hid Jewish people in the Benedictine convent in Vilnius, Lithuania. The convent was closed by the Russians. After the German conquest of Lithuania in June, 1941, the Benedictine convent was used by the Germans to store the books and documents they stole from the Lithuanians. In charge of the library and the document storage, Father Stakauskas hid Jewish people in the basement of the convent.

The centuries old building was a maze of cellars, garrets and corridors. The Germans asked Father Stakauskas to draw up a plan showing how the convent was to be used. Knowing that his Jewish friends would need a place to hide, he drew a careful plan without mentioning one end of the basement corridors. Hidden by large bookshelves built to conceal the end of the corridor, he invited his Jewish friends to live there. Twelve adults and children moved into the convent. They slept on straw mats. During the day, they had to be silent. Father Stakauskas brought them books from the Archives.

When the German and Lithuanian workers left the Archive at 4 o'clock in the afternoon, Sister Maria stamped on the floor three times. Then the hideout became a beehive of activity, washing, cleaning, cooking and conversation.

Father Stakauskas brought them food and visited with them every three or four days to cheer them. He told them "Either all of us will survive, or all of us will perish."

More than a thousand children were saved in the convents by Polish nuns. Matilda Getter the Mother Superior of the Poor Clares of the Franciscan Order rescued hundreds of Jewish children. Mother Maria Stanislas Polotynska, the Mother Superior of the Ursuline Mother house actively rescued Jewish children from arrest. The Grey Ursuline nuns were also involved in rescue activities.

Archbishop Andrii Szeptytyki in the Ukraine, raised his voice in protest of the involvement of Ukrainians in anti-Jewish actions. "Honest people should turn their backs on local murderers whose hands are covered with innocent blood," he publicly declared. The Archbishop saved the lives of 150 children and fifteen Rabbis by giving them asylum.

There were many other priests and nuns involved in rescue, but unfortunately their stories are not known. The Second World War, which saw the destiny of many groups linked in suffering, was a horrible time for dedicated

Catholics as well as Jews. One hundred and eight priests and nuns were beatified by Pope John Paul II, half of whom died through torture or execution in concentration camps. Their stories need to be remembered. They are a light in the darkness of the Holocaust. Their deeds not only saved lives, but proved that goodness can prevail in the darkest of times.

The Yad Vashem created the "Garden of the Righteous" to honor the heroic deeds of righteous people. Trees have been planted in their names, medals snd certificates have been given them or their representatives. The inscription on the medal reads "Whoever saves a single soul, it is as if he had saved the whole world."

The Catholic church has also honored them. .

References:

Gilbert, Martin (2003) *The Righteous: Unsung Heroes of the Holocaust*. Toronto, Ontario: Key Porter Books.

Gitelman, Zvi (ed) (1997) *Bitter Legacy: Confronting the Holocaust in the USSR.* Bloomington, Indiana: Indiana University Press, 1997.

Paldiel, Mordecai (1993*) The Path of the Righteous: Gentile Rescuers of Jews During The Holocaust.* Hoboken, N..J.: KTAV Publishing House.   .

Terms and Definitions.

World War II (1939-1945)

World War II began in 1939 with the invasion of Poland. Britain declared war on Germany in September .In 1940, the Germans invaded the Netherlands, Belgium, France and Luxembourg. US entered the war after the attack on Pearl Harbor by the Japanese in December 1941. The war ended in 1945 with the defeat of the Germans in May and the Japanese in September.

About the Holocaust

The persecution of Jewish people began when Hitler became the dictator of Germany in 1933. Nazi racial laws deprived Jews if citizenship, stripped of their rights and robbed them of their possessions. The first action against the Jews was the boycott of Jewish shops in April 1933, followed by book burnings and anti-Jewish laws. In November, 1938, Krystallnacht, the Night of Broken glass took place. Jewish shops were destroyed.

123

When World War II began in 1939, Jewish people were forced to wear the Star of David. In eastern Europe, they were robbed of their homes and belongings and forced to live in ghettoes. Beginning in 1940, Jews in all occupied countries were arrested and deported to concentration camps. Six death camps were set up in occupied Poland in 1941 and in 1942, the merciless killing of Jews in gas chambers was underway. Jewish people were also slaughtered by Nazi troops in occupied countries.

Prison Camps

Prison camps were set up shortly after Hitler took power in 1933, and were massively increased during the war. There were three types of camps:

1. Death camps: The main purpose of these camps were the killing of prisoners. The main camps were Auschwitz-Birkenau, Belzec, Chelmno, Majdanek, Sobibor, and Treblinka.

2. Concentration Camps

3. Work or Labor Camps: Prisoner were forced to work for the Nazis. They were slave laborers.

The Einsatzgruppen: paramilitary German units whose purpose was to liquidate (murder) Jews and other enemies of the Nazis Reich in occupied countries. Primarily responsible for killing of Russian Jews and the slaughter of Poles.

The Gestapo

The Gestapo were the German secret police.

Ghettoes: designated areas in European cities and towns in which Jews were forced to live. People lived in very crowded conditions.

The SS, the Schutzstaffel

The SS was created to be Hitler's bodyguard. They swore absolute loyalty to Hitler. SS troops ran and guarded the concentration camps and put infantry and armoured divisions into the field. The head of the SS was Heinrich Himmler, one of the most powerful men in Nazi Germany. The Gestapo (secret police) were also under Himmler's command.

5,962, 129 Jewish people were murdered. More than a million were young children. , 63% of European Jews were killed.

In Poland, 3,000,000 (91%)

In Hungary 596,000 (74%)

In France 200,000 (22%)

In Belgium, 36,800 (45%)

In Italy, 7,680 (17%)

References

Braham, Randolph L. (1994) *The Politics of Genocide: The Holocaust in Hungary,* vols. I & II, New York: Columbia University Press.

De Lubac, Henri, *Christian Resistance to Antisemitism: Memories from 1940-1944,* (1988) Ignatius Press, San Francisco.

Gallagher, J.P.(1967) *The Scarlet Pimpernel of the Vatican,* New York: Coward- McCann Inc.

Gitelman, Zvi (Ed) (1997) *Bitter Legacy: Confronting The Holocaust in the USSR.* Bloomington, Indiana, Indiana University Press.

Gilbert, Martin. (2003) *The Righteous: Unsung Heroes of the Holocaust,* Toronto, Canada: Key Porter Books.

Hertzer, Ivo (ed) (1987) *Refuge: Rescue of Jews During The Holocaust.* Washington D.C.: The Catholic University Press.

Klarsfeld, Serge (1984) *The Children of Izieu: A Human Tragedy*. Harry N. Abrams, Inc. New York.

Kurek,Ewa, (1997) *Your Life Is Worth Mine: How Polish Nuns Saved Hundreds of Jewish Children in German-Occupied Poland, 1939-1945,* NY:Hippocrene Books Inc.

Lapide, P. (1967) *Three Popes and The Jews: Pope Pius XII Did Not Remain Silent*. New York: Hawthorn Books.

Lapomarda, Rev. Vincent A.(1983)   Five Heroic Catholics of the Holocaust and The Cardinal of the Persecuted Jews. Yad Vashem Studies, Vol.15.

Leboucher, Ferdinand, (1969) *Incredible Mission*. NY: Doubleday and Company.

Marchione, Sister Margherita,(1997) *Yours Is A Precious Witness: Memoirs of Jews and Catholics in Wartime Italy,* Mahwah, NJ: Paulist Press

Paldiel, Mordecai, (1993) *The Path of the Righteous: Gentile Recuers of Jews During The Holocaust,* KTAV Publishing House , NJ: Hoboken.

Paldiel, Mordecai (2002) "Abducted From The Hands of the Aggressor: The Rescue of Jewish Chldren in Belgium. Yad Vashem Quarterly Magazine, Vol. 30, p.5.

Ramati, Alexander, (1978) While The Pope Kept Silent: Assisi and the Nazi Occupation (as told by Padre Rufino Nicacci) London, England: Geroge Allen and Unwin

Rychlak, Ronald J. (2000) *Hitler, the War and The Pope,* Columbia, Missouri: Genesis Press.

Schmidt, Maria (1987)"Action of Margit Slachta to Rescue Slovakian Jews." Danubian Historical Studies, 1,Vol : 58; G. Rocca, col. 1434 - 1435.

Zielinski, Father Zygmunt.(2000) "Nuns Who Saved Polish Jews." National Catholic Register.

Zuccotti, Susan,(1993) *The Holocaust, the French and the Jews*, Basic Books, NY (Division of Harper Collins.

Documentation Centers:

Catholic Holocaust Education Center website (Seton Hill University)

Yad Vashem Documentation Center, Israel. .

Sally M. Rogow   **BIBLIOGRAPHY**

Recent Book For Young People

Rogow, S.M. (2003) *Faces of Courage: Young Heroes of World War II.* Vancouver, B.C. Granville Island Publishing.

Books For Teachers

Rogow, S.M. (1997) *Language, Literacy and Children with Special Needs.* Toronto, Canada, Pippin Publishing.

Rogow, S.M. (2000) "Communication and Language: Issues and Concerns" *The Light House Handbook on Vision Impairment and Vision Rehabilitation.* Vol.2. New York, New York: Oxford University press.

Rogow, S.M. (1988) *Helping the visually impaired child with developmental problems: Effective practice in home, school and community.* NY: Teachers College Press, Columbia University.

Rogow, S.M. & Hass J. (!993) *Shared Moments: Learning Games for Young Children with Disabilities.* Greensboro, NC: Tudor Publishers.

133

Winzer, M. Rogow, S.M., David, C. (1986) *Exceptional children in Canada*. Toronto, Prentice Hall.

Printed in the United States
34361LVS00007B/44

9 780976 721161